Expository Nuggets
from
1 Corinthians

Stuart Briscoe Expository Outlines series

Expository Nuggets for Today's Christians
Expository Nuggets from Genesis and Exodus
Expository Nuggets from Psalms and Proverbs
Expository Nuggets from the Gospels
Expository Nuggets from 1 Corinthians
Expository Nuggets from the Epistles

Expository Nuggets
from
1 Corinthians

Stuart Briscoe Expository Outlines

D. Stuart Briscoe

Baker Books

A Division of Baker Book House Co
Grand Rapids, Michigan 49516

© 1995 by D. Stuart Briscoe

Published by Baker Books
a division of Baker Book House Company
P.O. Box 6287, Grand Rapids, MI 49516-6287

Printed in the United States of America

ISBN 0-8010-9006-7

Contents

Preface

Outlines and skeletons are quite similar. Sermons without outlines tend to "flop around" like bodies without bones. But bones without flesh are not particularly attractive; neither are outlines without development. The outlines presented in this book are nothing more than skeletal for a very good reason. I have no desire to produce ready-made sermons for pastors who need to develop their own, but on the other hand I recognize that many busy pastors who find sermon preparation time hard to come by may at least use them as a foundation for their own study, meditation, and preaching. They can add flesh to the bones; they can add development to structure. All the sermons based on these outlines have been preached during the last twenty-two years of my ministry at Elmbrook Church in Milwaukee, Wisconsin, and as one might expect, they vary in style and substance—not to mention quality! I trust, however, that they all seek to teach the Word and apply it to the culture to which they were preached, and if they help another generation of preachers as they "preach the Word," I will be grateful.

1

Getting Things Straight

1 Corinthians 1:1-9

The Corinthian church was both a marvel and a mess, like many churches and many lives. Paul's intention in his first epistle to the Corinthians is to preserve the marvel and clear up the mess: praiseworthy intentions but fraught with problems.

I. Why bother getting things straight?
    A. Because of the strategic position of the church
        Note: "church of God at Corinth" (v. 2)
    B. Because of the special purposes of Christ shown in his:
        1. Calling work—"called saints" (v. 2)
        2. Confirming work—"testimony confirmed in you" (v. 6)
        3. Charismatic work—"behind in no gift" (v. 7)
        4. Climactic work—"the coming of our Lord" (v. 7)
    C. Because of the spiritual privileges of Christians
        1. Realizing God's plan—"will of God" (v. 1)

2. Relating to God's people—"theirs and ours" (v. 2)
3. Relying on God's promises—"God is faithful" (v. 9)

II. How do we go about getting things straight?
  A. By giving credit where it is due
    1. To God—"the grace of God" (v. 4)
    2. To those who demonstrate his grace (vv. 5–7; 11:2)
  B. By giving criticism where it is necessary
    1. Incompatibility that is not being resolved (1:10)
    2. Irresponsibility that is not being recognized (3:1–2; Heb. 5:11–13)
    3. Immorality that is not being rebuked (1 Cor. 5:1)
    4. Illiteracy that is not being rectified (3:16; 6:9, 15, 19)
  C. By giving clarification where it is needed
    1. Concerning marital matters (7:1–40)
    2. Concerning social matters (8:1–10:33)
    3. Concerning ecclesiastical matters (11:1–14:40)
    4. Concerning theological matters (15:1–50)
    5. Concerning financial matters (16:1–24)

2

Division in the Church

1 Corinthians 1:10–16

The church at Corinth was not living up to her potential. Differences had led to quarreling, and divisions were threatening. Paul spoke to the issue with great urgency and intensity.

I. The curse of division
   A. It dishonors the name of Christ
   B. It dismantles the work of Christ
   C. It disgusts the enemies of Christ
   D. It discourages the servants of Christ
   E. It disorganizes the church of Christ
   F. It disappoints the Spirit of Christ

II. The cause of division
   A. Strategy of Satan (2 Cor. 2:11)
      1. To exploit
      2. To explode

B. Stupidity of saints
   1. Making convictions into contentions (1 Cor. 1:11)
   2. Making personalities into parties (v. 12)
   3. Making molehills into mountains (3:1–3)

III. The cure of division
   A. Clarify the issues (1:11)
   B. Identify the problems (3:3)
   C. Rectify the ills (1:10)
      1. Speaking
      2. Thinking
      3. Deciding
      4. Healing
   D. Specify the priorities (v. 13)
      1. Battles don't build the body
      2. The cross of Christ is still central
      3. The master matters more than men

3

The Cross of Christ

1 Corinthians 1:17–18

The stark simplicity of the message of Christ was under attack in Corinth as it is around the world today. Paul reminded the Corinthians and he reminds us that we deviate from the cross at our peril.

  I. The preaching of the cross
     A. The significance of the message
        1. The cross–design, not disaster (Heb. 12:2, 22–24)
        2. The cross–honor, not humiliation (Phil. 2:5–11)
        3. The cross–triumph, not tragedy (Col. 1:12–20)
     B. The significance of the method (1 Cor. 1:17)
        1. Preaching not superseded by philosophy
        2. Baptism not superior to preaching

 II. The perishing and the cross
     A. The condition of the perishing
        1. They are disintegrating (Luke 5:37)
        2. They are deteriorating (John 6:27)

        3. They are disorientated (Luke 15:4)
        4. They face destruction (Acts 27:34)
    B. The conviction of the perishing
        1. To them the cross is nonsense
        2. To them the crucifixion is a scandal

III. The power of the cross
    A. The initial power of the cross
        1. To rescue the perishing (John 3:16)
        2. To reassure the doubting (5:24)
    B. The continual power of the cross
        1. As the believer's acclamation (Gal. 6:14)
        2. As the believer's attitude (Matt. 10:38)
        3. As the believer's activity (Gal. 5:24)

4

Sense and Nonsense

1 Corinthians 1:19-25

Confusion reigns in our world. The cause of this confusion is a mystery to many people. The Bible says it is caused in part by God's sense being regarded by man's nonsense, and man's sense being dismissed as nonsense by God.

I. The sense that is nonsense—"God made foolish the wisdom of this world" (v. 20)
   A. The birth of worldly wisdom (Rom. 1:18–23)
      1. Resistance to righteousness of God (v. 18)
      2. Rejection of revelation of God (vv. 19–20)
      3. Refusal to recognize God (v. 21)–"professing to be wise, they became fools" (v. 22)
   B. The growth of worldly wisdom
      1. The practical approach—"the Jews seek signs" (1 Cor. 1:22a)
         a. Materialism
         b. Secularism

    2. The philosophical approach—"the Greeks seek wisdom" (v. 22b)
      a. Idealism
      b. Naturalism
      c. Existentialism
  C. The death of worldly wisdom
    1. It cannot meet man's deepest needs (v. 20)
    2. It cannot lead to man's highest end (v. 21)
    3. It cannot heal the world's greatest ills (James 3:13–18)

II. The nonsense that makes sense—"Christ crucified . . . an offense . . . and foolishness" (1 Cor. 1:23)
  A. The scope of God's wisdom
    1. It offers salvation to all who believe (v. 21)
    2. It calls to God all who respond (v. 24)
    3. It unites in Christ all who are saved (v. 24a)
    4. It releases blessing to all who receive (v. 24b)
  B. The scandal of God's wisdom
    1. An insult to the practical
    2. A nonsense to the sophisticated
  C. The scale of the wisdom of God (v. 25)
    1. God's foolishness solves more than man's wisdom
    2. God's weakness achieves more than man's power

5

More Foolishness

1 Corinthians 1:26-31

God insists on being himself and doing things his own way. Man doesn't like this very much and thinks it foolishness. But he needs to be careful because "the foolishness of God is wiser than men."

I. The plan God chose to adopt
   A. His insistence on revealing his glory
      1. In his unique character (Isa. 43:11; Deut. 4:35)
      2. In his unique creation (Gen. 1:26; Ps. 45:1)
   B. His resistance to sharing his glory
      1. Angelic attempts (Isa. 14:12-17)
      2. Human attempts (Gen. 3:5; Exod. 20:1-5; Acts 12:23; 1 Cor. 1:29-31)
   C. His persistence in demonstrating his glory (Phil. 2:6-11)
      1. Incarnation
      2. Crucifixion
      3. Resurrection
      4. Coronation

II. The procedures God chose to employ
   A. His call contradicted human reason
      Note: not many wise, powerful, or noble (1 Cor. 1:26)
   B. His choice confounded human resources (v. 27)
     1. Children of Israel confounded Egyptian pharaoh
     2. Cross of shame confounded Jewish elite
     3. Church of Christ confounded Roman empire
     4. Christians of today confound political systems

III. The people God chose to use (vv. 30–31)
   A. Those who are related to him
     1. Of him
     2. In Christ
   B. Those who are right with him
     1. Righteousness
     2. Sanctification
     3. Redemption
   C. Those who are rejoicing in him (see Jer. 9:23–24)

6

Talking Sense

1 Corinthians 2:1-8

Paul's arrival in Corinth heralded the start of a new life for many people. Because of his ministry, many turned to the Lord and the church was founded. Nevertheless, things were not going as well as they might have, and Paul reminds the Corinthians how they got started and how they need to go on. He talks a lot of sense to them.

I. Talking sense—what to say
   A. The testimony of God (v. 1); e.g., the ark of testimony (Exod. 16:33–34; Heb. 9:4)
     1. The ark—the presence of God (Exod. 25:21–22)
     2. The tablets—the preeminence of God (v. 16)
     3. The pot—the provision of God (vv. 33–34)
     4. The rod—the power of God (Heb. 9:4)
   B. The power of God (1 Cor. 2:5)
     1. The power to resurrect (6:14)
     2. The power to reign (15:24)
     3. The power to reveal (2 Cor. 4:7)
     4. The power to restore (12:9)

C. The wisdom of God (1 Cor. 2:7)
   1. Conceived before the world
   2. Concealed until Christ
   3. Consummated in glory
   4. Contradicted by this age (v. 6)

II. Talking sense—how to say it
   A. By means of declaration (v. 1)
      1. Reasons
      2. Persuaded
      3. Testified (Acts 18:4–5)
         Note: 1 Corinthians 2:1
   B. By means of determination (v. 2)
      1. Not to compromise the message (v. 2)
      2. Not to capitulate to fear (v. 3)
   C. By means of demonstration (v. 4)
      1. A messenger anointed by the Spirit
      2. A message authenticated by the Spirit

III. Talking sense—what to expect (v. 5)
   A. People's faith will reject human wisdom
   B. People's faith will rest in divine power

7

Spiritual Discernment

1 Corinthians 2:9–14

The things of God are a mystery to mankind. This means that we are seriously deficient in our understanding of God, his purposes, and his plans. But God has taken steps to give us spiritual discernment so that the mystery may become clear.

I. The possibilities of spiritual discernment
   A. What God has prepared for those who love him (Rom. 8:28)
      1. He has prepared salvation (Luke 2:31)
      2. He has prepared a kingdom (Matt. 25:34)
      3. He has prepared a position (20:23)
   B. What God has prepared for those who resist him
      1. He has prepared for the devil (25:41–46)
      2. He has prepared for the unprepared

II. The principles of spiritual discernment
   A. The activity of the Holy Spirit
      1. Exploring the things of God (1 Cor. 2:10)
      2. Expressing the things of God (v. 10)

B. The attitude of human beings
   1. Rejecting the spirit of the world (v. 12)
   2. Receiving the Spirit of God (v. 12)
   3. Relating the things of God (v. 13)
      a. Through Spirit-given words
      b. Through Spirit-imparted truths

III. The problems of spiritual discernment
   A. The problem of the natural man
      1. He doesn't receive illumination
      2. He doesn't respect illumination
      3. He doesn't recognize illumination
         a. Eye
         b. Ear
         c. Heart
   B. The problem of the carnal man
      1. Inadequate appetite
      2. Inadequate appreciation

8

Belief and Behavior

1 Corinthians 2:14-3:4

The problems of the church are called people. The chief problem with people is matching belief and behavior. We all need help in this area.

I. The natural person (v. 14)
   Note: "natural"–Greek *psuchikos*
   A. What the natural person believes
      1. He believes spiritual things are nonsense
      2. He believes spiritual truth should be rejected
      3. He believes only what is observable by sense (see v. 9)
   B. How the natural person behaves (James 3:15; Jude 18–19)
      In a manner that is:
      1. Sensual
      2. Satanic
      3. Secular
      4. Sinful
      5. Shameful

II. The spiritual person (1 Cor. 2:15–16)
    Note: "spiritual"–Greek *pneumatikos*
    A. What the spiritual person believes
        1. He believes the truth the Spirit teaches (v. 10)
        2. He receives the life the Spirit offers (v. 12)
        3. He achieves the relationship the Spirit provides (vv. 15–16)
    B. How the spiritual person behaves
        1. With great discernment (v. 15a)
        2. With great distinction (v. 15b)
        3. With great discipline (14:37; Gal. 6:1)

III. The carnal person (1 Cor. 3:1–3)
    Note: "carnal"–Greek *sarkikos*
    A. What the carnal person believes
        1. He believes what the spiritual person believes
        2. He receives what the spiritual person receives
    B. How the carnal person behaves
        1. Inconsistently–he believes as the spiritual person but behaves as the natural person
        2. Immaturely (v. 1)
            a. Inability (v. 2)
            b. Incompatibility (v. 3)
            c. Irresponsibility (Heb. 5:11–13)
            d. Instability (Eph. 4:14)

9

Childlike and Childish

1 Corinthians 3:1-4

The carnal person believes like a spiritual person and acts like a natural person. He is a mature man who behaves like a big baby. Being a baby is fine for babies but a disaster for adults. There's a difference between being childlike and childish.

I. The beauty of childlikeness
   A. As an illustration of the way to glory (Matt. 18:3-4)
      1. Humility
      2. Trust
      3. Transparency
   B. As an indication of the way to grow (2 Tim. 3:14-17)
      1. Child
      2. Man
      3. Mature
      4. Equipped

II. The tragedy of childishness
   A. Because of what it is
     1. Evidence of arrested development
     2. Evidence of neglected principles
   B. Because of what it does
     1. It shows immaturity (see 1 Cor. 13:11)
       a. The talk it engages in
       b. The thoughts it entertains
       c. The things it enjoys
     2. It shows irresponsibility (see Heb. 5:12–14)
       a. Irresponsibility in action (v. 12)
       b. Irresponsibility in assimilation (v. 13)
       c. Irresponsibility in attention (v. 14)
     3. It shows inability (1 Cor. 3:1–2)
       a. Inability to discern (v. 1)
       b. Inability to digest (v. 2)
     4. It shows incompatibility (vv. 3–4)
       a. In personal situations (v. 3)
       b. In party strife (v. 4)
     5. It shows instability (Eph. 4:14)
       a. Instability in daily living
       b. Instability in doctrinal direction

III. The remedy for carnality
   A. Growth requires good food (Luke 4:4)
   B. Growth requires healthy exercise (Gal. 5:16, 24)
   C. Growth requires fresh air (Matt. 26:41)
   D. Growth requires regular rest (11:28–30)

10

God's Garden

1 Corinthians 3:5-9

There are many ways of looking at the church. "God's husbandry are ye" (v. 9) is one of them. It means God's garden. The Corinthian church did not always fit this description. Paul's letter endeavors to rectify this.

I. God's desire for a garden
   A. A place to enjoy the fruits of holiness (Rom. 6:22)
   B. A place to experience the fragrance of Christ (2 Cor. 2:15)
   C. A place to express the flowering of righteousness (Ps. 92:12-15)
   D. A place to exult in the freshness of worship (96:9)

II. God's design for his garden
   A. The work that needs to be done
      1. Preparation
         a. Plowing
         b. Planting

    2. Germination
      a. Life
      b. Growth
    3. Cultivation
      a. Watering
      b. Weeding
  B. The workers that need to be working
    1. Status–"ministers"= *diakonoi* (1 Cor. 3:5; see
      Matt. 20:28; Mark 1:13, 31; Rom. 12:7; 13:6)
    2. Skills–"as the Lord gave" (1 Cor. 3:5)
    3. Salary–"reward according to labor" (v. 8)
    4. Strength–"laborers together with God" (v. 9)
      a. Unity (v. 8)
      b. Union (v. 9)
  C. The work that God must do–he "makes things
    grow" (v.7)

III. God's dissatisfaction with his garden
  A. Because of barrennesses (see Matt. 21:18–19)–
    the absence of what should be (see I.)
  B. Because of bitterness–the presence of what
    shouldn't be
    1. Worker problems
      a. Idle workers (20:6)
      b. Incompatible workers (v. 11)
      c. Incompetent workers (v. 7)
    2. Watering problems (e.g., see Acts 6:1)
    3. Weeding problems (e.g., see 1 Cor. 5:1–2)

11

God's Building

1 Corinthians 3:9-15

Paul's objective in writing to the Corinthian church was to get it operating more like a church. Part of his strategy was to give the people a higher view of the church. "God's building are ye," he said.

    I. The building (v. 9)
       A. The place that God owns–"God's building"
       B. The place where God operates–"God is building"
       C. The place that God occupies–"God's temple"

   II. The foundation (vv. 10–11)
       A. Limited to Jesus Christ
         1. Whose love we return (1 John 4:19)
         2. Whose law we revere (Gal. 6:2)
         3. Whose life we reflect (Phil. 2:13–15)
       B. Laid by the apostles
         1. To start the building
         2. To support the building
         3. To shape the building

III. The architect (1 Cor. 3:10)
   Note: "master builder"–Greek *architekton*
   A. Called
   B. Equipped
   C. Skilled

IV. The builders
   A. Careful about what they build
      1. Themselves (Acts 20:32; Jude 20)
      2. Each other (Rom. 14:19)
      3. The church (Acts 9:31)
   B. Careful about where they build
      Note: build upon (1 Cor. 3:10)
   C. Careful about how they build

V. The materials (v. 12)
   Note: contrast between Greek temples and slum dwellings
   A. The identity of the materials–gold, silver, etc.
   B. The quality of the materials
      1. What sort it is (v. 13)
      2. How real it is (v. 14)

VI. The inspection
   Note: this fire is for judgment, not purgation
   A. The continual tests of adversity
   B. The final test of eternity

VII. The remuneration (vv. 14–15)
   A. Eternal salvation is a gift of grace
   B. Effective service is a labor of love
      1. Those who serve will be rewarded
      2. Those who don't will be embarrassed

12

God's Temple

1 Corinthians 3:16-17

The Greeks in Corinth knew about the temple of Aphrodite. The Jews were familiar with the temple of Solomon. But Paul had taught them about God's temple—the church—and they had forgotten. So he reminded them.

    I. God's temple defined
       A. A meeting place
          1. The God who meets with people
            a. His will (1:1)
            b. His grace (v. 3)
            c. His faithfulness (v. 9)
            d. His power (v. 18)
            e. His wisdom (v. 24)
          2. The people who meet with God
            a. Those who want to be washed (6:9–11)
            b. Those who want to worship (1 Kings 8:62–66)
            c. Those who want to work (Ezek. 47:1–12)

   B. A dwelling place
      1. The unique person who dwells
         a. The Holy Spirit of revelation (1 Cor. 2:10)
         b. The Holy Spirit of regeneration (v. 4)
      2. The unique purpose of his dwelling
         a. His "growth" ministry (Acts 13:2–3; Eph. 4:3–16)
         b. His "grace" ministry (Acts 1:8)
         c. His "gift" ministry (1 Cor. 12:1–11)
         d. His "governing" ministry (Acts 15:28; 20:28)
         e. His "guidance" ministry (John 16:13)
         f. His "glorifying" ministry (Eph. 5:18–19)
   C. A holy place (1 Cor. 3:17)
      1. "Set apart" to God's person
      2. "Set apart" to God's program

II. God's temple defiled (v. 17)
   A. The possibility of defilement
      1. By refusing to meet with God
      2. By resisting the ministry of the Spirit
      3. By reneging on commitment to the Lord
   B. The penalty for defilement
      1. Punishment will fit the crime
      2. Punishment will not contradict (v. 15)
   C. The purging of defilement (e.g., John 2:13–17)

13

Dealing with Deception

1 Corinthians 3:18-23

Deception is an art as old as Eden. Its highly sophisticated use in the world today is something everyone must learn to combat. "Let no man deceive himself" (v. 18).

I. Recognize the power of deceptive forces
  A. The forces of deception
    1. The power of sin to deceive (Heb. 3:13)
    2. The power of Satan to deceive (2 Cor. 11:3)
    3. The power of self to deceive (Gal. 6:3; James 1:22)
    4. The power of society to deceive
      a. Contemporary thinking (1 Cor. 3:18)
      b. Contemporary standards (v. 19)
      c. Contemporary interests (Matt. 13:22)
      d. Contemporary values (1 Cor. 3:21a)
  B. The fruits of deception
    1. Mistaken philosophies—folly for wisdom
    2. Misplaced trust—self for God
    3. Miscalculated values—man for "all things"

  II. Resist the pressure of deceptive factors
      A. Let no man deceive himself (v. 18)
          1. By seeing himself in the light of reality
          2. By setting himself in the place of blessing
      B. Let no man deceive you (Eph. 5:6)
          1. By reviewing what is said
          2. By rejecting what is "vain"

 III. Receive the plenitude of divine favor
      Note: "all things are yours" (1 Cor. 3:22) to enjoy
      (1 Tim. 6:17) for good (Rom. 8:28)
      A. The divine opportunities (1 Cor. 3:22)
          1. To be taught by the Lord–"Paul"
          2. To be true to the Lord–"world"
          3. To be tested by the Lord–"life"
          4. To triumph because of the Lord–"death"
          5. To take from the Lord–"things present"
          6. To trust in the Lord–"things to come"
      B. The divine obligations
          1. You are the Lord's
          2. Christ is God's

14

Understanding the Minister

1 Corinthians 4:1-6

Ministers of the gospel have a unique position to fill. The details of this are not always clear to either minister or congregation. This is a dangerous situation and can lead to great conflict as it did in Corinth. Remember: we will *all* stand at the judgment seat of Christ!

  I. The privileges of the ministry (v. 1)
    A. Ministers of Christ
       Note: "minister"–Greek *huperetes*, "under rower"
       1. One who applies Christ's orders (Matt. 5:25)
       2. One who assists Christ's actions (Luke 4:20)
       3. One who administers Christ's affairs (Acts 13:5)
    B. Stewards of mysteries
       Note: "steward"–Greek *oikonomos*, "manager of household" (see Luke 12:42; Romans 16:23)
       Managing the mystery of–
       1. Divine truth (Matt. 13:11)
       2. Divine purpose (Rom. 16:25)
       3. Divine promise (1 Cor. 15:51)
       4. Divine principle (Eph. 5:32)

     5. Divine power (Col. 1:27)

     Note also Titus 1:7; 1 Peter 4:10

II. The pressures of the ministry (1 Cor. 4:3–4)

  A. Congregational pressures

    1. Manipulation–tying the minister's hands

    2. Adulation–swelling the minister's head

    3. Antagonism–breaking the minister's heart

  B. Societal pressures

    Note: man's judgment–literally "man's day"

    1. Succumbing to popular demands

    2. Subscribing to popular opinion

  C. Personal pressures

    1. The danger of chronic introspection

    2. The danger of unrealistic expectations

III. The perspectives of the ministry

  A. Discount much congregational pressure

    Note: "very small thing" (v. 3)

    1. Because it is limited in understanding

    2. Because it is subjective in outlook

    3. Because it is more emotional than rational

      Note: "account"–Greek *logizomai,* literally "calculate"

  B. Discontinue much personal pressure

    1. Because it is incapable of accurate evaluation (v. 4)

    2. Because it is counter-productive

  C. Discover divine pressure (v. 5); "he that judges me is the Lord" (v. 4)

    1. He will expose the murky things

    2. He will examine the motivational things

    3. He will exalt the magnificent things

IV. The pleasures of the ministry

  A. Knowing that people are trying to understand

  B. Knowing that people are committed to undergird

  C. Knowing that people refuse to undercut

15

Spiritual Pride

1 Corinthians 4:6-21

God has let it be known that he "resists the proud" (1 Peter 5:5). He has told us that "pride comes before destruction" (Prov. 16:18). This was another of the Corinthians' problems. They were "puffed up" with the worst kind of pride—spiritual pride.

I. How spiritual pride can be expressed
   A. Through a "superiority complex" (v. 6)
      1. One against the other in comparison
      2. One against the other in hostility
   B. Through self-confidence (v. 18)
      1. We are independent of leadership
      2. Leadership is in awe of us
   C. Through special considerations (5:2)
      1. Principles don't apply to us
      2. We don't need discipline

II. How spiritual pride can be explained
   A. A little learning is a dangerous thing (8:1–2)
     1. When it masks ignorance
     2. When it produces dogmatism
   B. A lack of love (13:4)
     1. "Tears down" instead of "builds up"
     2. "Bends low" rather than "puffs up"
   C. A fleshly motivation (Col. 2:18)
     1. Through unapplied knowledge
     2. Through unheeded truth

III. How spiritual pride can be exposed
   A. By serious contemplation (1 Cor. 4:7)
     1. Who made me what I am?
     2. Who gave me what I have?
     3. Who deserves the glory?
   B. By honest confrontation (v. 8)
     1. Am I as complete as I pretend?
     2. Am I as rich as I suggest?
     3. Am I as victorious as I preach?
   C. By careful consideration (vv. 9–13)
     1. God's ways with his men (v. 9)
     2. God's grace in adversity (vv. 10–13)
     3. My response in comparison (vv. 10–13)

IV. How spiritual pride can be expelled
   A. By hearing God's word through others (v. 6)– literally, "learn by us to learn to live according to Scripture"
   B. By heeding God's warning through others (v. 14)
   C. By honoring God's work in others (v. 16)
   D. By humbling yourself before others

16

Spiritual Delusion

1 Corinthians 4:8-21

Delusion is belief in something contrary to fact or reality. It can be caused by deception, misconception, or false perception. Paul was convinced that the Corinthians were deluded about their own spirituality.

I. Some delusions of spirituality
   A. The causes of delusion
      1. Deception by the deceiver (Rev. 12:9)
      2. Misconception of the truth
         Note: 1 Corinthians 3:16; 5:6; 6:3, 9, 15–16, 19; 9:24
      3. False perception of facts
         Note: things aren't always what they seem
   B. The characteristics of delusion
      1. An inflated view of personal condition (4:8)
         a. Full
         b. Rich
         c. Reigning
            Note: Revelation 3:17

    2. An inconsistent application of personal position (1 Cor. 4:20)
       a. To profess the kingdom is inadequate
       b. To project the kingdom is imperative
         Note: James 2:14–20

II. Some demonstrations of reality
   A. Spiritual reality is seen in character (1 Cor. 4:9–10)
     1. Bearing personal indignities–"fools"
     2. Enduring physical exhaustion–"weak"
     3. Accepting social ostracism–"despised"
   B. Spiritual reality is seen in commitment (v. 11)
     1. The commitment of involvement
     2. The commitment of cost
   C. Spiritual reality is seen in control (vv. 12–13)
     1. The control that refuses to react
     2. The control that manages to respond
   D. Spiritual reality is seen in compassion (vv. 14–17)
     1. Loving practically
       a. Warm
       b. Beseech
       c. Sent
     2. Loving persistently
       Note: "I will come"
   E. Spiritual reality is seen in courage (v. 21)
     1. Courage to grasp the nettle
     2. Courage to do what's necessary

17

Church Discipline

1 Corinthians 5:1-13

"Church discipline" is the action taken by a fellowship against one of its members whose activities may be jeopardizing his own spiritual well-being and the life and testimony of the body.

    I. The application of church discipline
        A. Its necessity
            1. The deterioration of moral standards (vv. 1-2a)
                a. Contemporary thinking rather than biblical truth
                b. Confusion of liberty and laxity
                c. Contentment without discipline
            2. The insinuation of heretical teaching (Gal. 1:6-9; 2 John 7-11)
                a. By discovering what is basic
                b. By denying what is unacceptable
        B. Its objectives
            1. To restore the culprit
                a. By forcing him to recognize

            b. By encouraging him to respond
            c. By leading him to repentance
            d. By helping him to restoration
         2. To remind the careless (1 Tim. 5:20)
            a. That sin has consequences
            b. That the church is serious business
         3. To revive the church
            a. To a clearer projection of the character of God
            b. To a fuller proclamation of the gospel of Christ
            c. To a deeper production of the work of the Spirit
     C. Its practice
         1. Personal preparation (Gal. 6:1)
         2. Individual approach (Matt. 18:15)
         3. Team approach (v. 16; 1 Tim. 5:19; Titus 3:10–11)
         4. Congregational action (1 Cor. 5:4–5; see Matt. 18:17)
            a. In the name of the Lord Jesus (1 Cor. 5:4a)
            b. In the power of the Lord Jesus (v. 4b)
            c. For the day of the Lord Jesus (v. 5)

  II. The abuse of church discipline
     A. Tyranny
         1. Inquisition–the abuse of power
         2. Jan Hus –the martyr
         3. Galileo–the triumph of prejudice
     B. Laxity
         1. Corinth
         2. Contemporary West
         3. Ecumenicalism
     C. Schism–discipline not according to principle

III. The alternative to church discipline–self-discipline (vv. 6–13)
     A. Christ is our Passover
     B. Let us keep the feast
     C. Purge out the old leaven

18

Spring Cleaning

1 Corinthians 5:6–8

Churches, like houses, need a regular spring cleaning. This time had come for the Corinthians. Paul used the analogy of the Feast of the Passover to urge them to "purge out the leaven."

   I. The historical incident (Exod. 12:1–13)
      A. Instituted in Egypt
      B. Commemorated in Sinai (Num. 9:1–5)
      C. Observed in Jerusalem (2 Chron. 35:1–19; Ezra 6:19–22)
      D. Celebrated in dispersion

  II. The spiritual illustration (1 Cor. 5:7)
      Note: "Christ our Passover lamb has been sacrificed"
      A. The lamb must be slain (Exod. 12:5)
         1. Without blemish
         2. First year
         3. From the fold

B. The blood must be applied (v. 7)
1. Lintel
2. Doorposts   *Good*
3. Not threshold
C. The flesh must be eaten (vv. 8–10)
1. Roast
2. Unleavened
3. Bitter herbs
4. In entirety
D. The loins must be girded (vv. 8–10)
1. Loins
2. Unleavened
3. Bitter herbs
4. In entirety
E. The Lord must be trusted (v. 13; Heb. 11:28)

III. The practical implication (1 Cor. 5:6–8)
A. Purge the yeast because–
1. A little leaven goes a long way (v. 6)
2. Unleavened dough hates leaven (v. 7)
3. Leaven is malicious and wicked (v. 8)
B. Keep the feast
1. With sincerity of motive (v. 8)
2. With reality of action (v. 8)

19

Separation of Church

1 Corinthians 5:9-13

Separation of church and state is a matter of some importance to many believers. But the separation of which Paul wrote was quite different–the separation of church and sin.

I. The definition of church separation
   A. Separation defined
      1. "Not to company with" (vv. 9, 11)
      2. "Be not unequally yoked" (2 Cor. 6:14–17)
         a. No fellowship
         b. No communion
         c. No concord
         d. No part
         e. No agreement
   B. Sin defined
      1. Sexual sins
         a. Fornication (1 Cor. 5:9)
         b. Adultery (6:9)
         c. Homosexuality (v. 9)
      2. Social sins
         a. Covetousness (5:10)

      b. Extortion (v. 10)
      c. Drunkenness (6:10)
    3. Spiritual sins
      a. Idolatry

II. The design of church separation
  A. To underscore the seriousness of sin
    1. Sin bars entrance to the kingdom (6:9)
    2. Sin blights effectiveness of the kingdom
  B. To undergird the sanctification of sinners (v. 11)
    1. By removing contradictory forces (2 Cor. 6:14–17)
      a. Unbelief
      b. Unrighteousness
      c. Darkness
      d. Belial
      e. Idols
    2. By revealing contrasting factors
      a. Righteousness
      b. Light
      c. Christ
      d. Belief
      e. Temple of God

III. The degree of church separation
  A. Too much leads to isolation (1 Cor. 5:10)–"go out of the world"
  B. Too little leads to infection–"a little leaven"

20

Saints and Sinners

1 Corinthians 6:1–11

I. The state of the sinner
   A. The decalogue of God
      1. God's choice in creation
      2. God's choice in covenant (Exod. 20:6)
         a. A covenant of loving-kindness
         b. A covenant of loving obedience
   B. The defiance of mankind (1 Cor. 6:9–10)
      1. Idolaters, revelers don't love God adequately
      2. Fornicators, adulterers, homosexuals, drunkards don't love themselves adequately
      3. Thieves, coveters, swindlers don't love their neighbors adequately
      4. This amounts to covenant breaking
   C. The destruction of society
      1. The loss of spiritual values–before God
      2. The loss of personal worth
      3. The loss of societal experiences

II. The salvation of the sinner
   A. The "how" of salvation
      1. By acknowledging responsibility
        Note: sin and sickness debate; e.g., homosexual, drunkard
      2. By demonstrating repentance
        Note: "Such were some of you" (v. 11)
      3. By accepting redemption
        a. You were washed
        b. You were sanctified
        c. You were justified
   B. The "who" of salvation
      1. The Lord Jesus Christ
      2. The Spirit of God

III. The status of the saint
   Note: *saint* is the word for a washed, sanctified, justified sinner
   A. Settled in the kingdom
   B. Set apart for God

IV. The style of a saint
   A. The convictions of a saint
      Saints have—
      1. Rejected sinful lifestyle
      2. Accepted restrictive lifestyle (v. 1)
      3. Responded to responsible lifestyle (vv. 2–3)
   B. The concerns of a saint
      1. Saints prefer to be defrauded than defeated (v. 7)
      2. Saints prefer to be wronged than to wrong (v. 8)

21

Liberty and Libertines

1 Corinthians 6:12

"All things are lawful" appears to have been a Corinthian slogan. Paul agrees; in fact, he may have taught it. But the Corinthians had misinterpreted liberty and had become libertines. Liberty is no more intended to produce libertines than that which is permissible should be used to produce permissiveness.

    I. The law of liberty
       A. The quest for freedom
          Note: man cannot get free from himself
          1. Political (Isa. 14:12)
          2. Personal (Gen. 3:1–5)
          3. Religious (4:1–8)
          4. Moral (6:1–7)
          5. Economic (vv. 1–7)
       B. The gift of freedom
          1. Traditional view of religious liberty
             a. Justification is the reward for sanctification

          b. Believed in paganism, Judaism, Catholicism, Protestant fundamentalism

   2. Biblical view of religious liberty

          a. Sanctification is the result of justification

          b. Justification is the gift of grace

          c. So justified man is free from conditions

          d. So "all things are lawful" (see John 8:31–36; Galatians 5:1)

II. The limitations of liberty

   A. Compulsory limitations

      1. Freedom has an environment; e.g., fish in water, man in oxygen

      2. Christian freedom is "in the Lord"

          a. So Lordship of Christ is basic

          b. Sin is bondage, so freedom to sin is contradiction

   B. Voluntary limitations

      1. If the "permissible" is not profitable (1 Cor. 6:12; see 7:35; 10:33)

      2. If the "permissible" is too powerful (6:12; see Heb. 12:1; note "weights and sin")

      3. If the "permissible" is not productive (1 Cor. 10:23)

III. The lifestyle of the liberated

   A. In contrast to the libertine

   B. In conformity to the Lord

      1. Lordship, not liberty, is the governing factor

      2. Love, not license, is the motivating force

22

Glorifying God in the Body

1 Corinthians 6:13-20

Bodies can be a problem. Especially if they are governed by pagan philosophy. Christian theology, however, has much to say about the body. Not least that it should be used to glorify God.

I. The body–made by God
   A. Body and spirit = man (Gen. 2:7)
   B. Body and spirit influence each other
   C. Body will be vacated by spirit (Eccles. 12:7)
   D. Body will return to dust (Ps. 104:29)
   E. Body will be raised (1 Cor. 6:14)

II. The body–misused by man
   A. Stomachs and food (v. 13)
      1. Made for each other
      2. Both are temporary
   B. Sex and fornication (v. 13)
      Note: Greek and Corinthian attitudes toward these things

1. Food may satisfy the stomach's appetite
2. Fornication must not satisfy the sexual appetite
3. Because the body is more than stomach
4. The Lord is to motivate the body

III. The body—the means of glorifying God
    A. By clear understanding of the body's function
        1. As made for the Lord and the Lord for it (v. 13)
        2. As member of Christ (v. 15)
        3. As temple of the Holy Spirit (v. 19)
        4. As possession of God (v. 20)
    B. By careful discipline of the body's activities
        1. From a negative point of view—flee fornication (v. 18)
        2. From a positive point of view
           a. By doing what it was made to do
           b. By keeping it a credit to Christ, its head
           c. By demonstrating the indwelling presence
           d. By drawing attention to the owner, not the tenant

23

Human Sexuality

1 Corinthians 7:1-9

The Corinthians had raised a question about celibacy. Paul deals with it in the whole context of human sexuality.

    I. Sexuality in a pagan environment
       A. The Corinthians' approach
          1. Luxury
          2. Indulgence
          3. Hedonism
          4. Fornication (v. 2)
       B. The ascetic approach
          Note: asceticism means denial of physical or psychological desire to attain spiritual ideal or goal
          1. Olympic athletes
          2. Stoics
          3. Platonists
       C. The contemporary approach
          1. Contemporary Corinthianism
          2. Contemporary asceticism

II. Sexuality in a Christian experience
    A. Sexuality and the single person
        1. Celibacy is good (not better or best) (v. 1)
        2. Celibacy has benefits (vv. 26–34)
        3. Celibacy has disadvantages (v. 9)
    B. Sexuality and the married person
        1. Sexuality and stability (v. 2)–"his own," "her own"
        2. Sexuality and integrity (v. 3)–"due benevolence," literally "debt"
        3. Sexuality and mutuality (v. 4)–"authority"
        4. Sexuality and spirituality (v. 5)–"self-control," "Satan," "prayer"
        5. Sexuality and serenity (v. 9)–"burn"

III. Christian sexuality in a pagan world
    A. Involves obligation to biblical ethics
    B. Involves operation of Spirit's energy
    C. Involves opposition to godlessness

24

Marriages under Pressure

1 Corinthians 7:10-16

Christian marriage in pagan society is a challenge second to none. Mixed marriage in a pagan society is even more difficult. The Corinthians knew a lot about both and needed some clarification. The situation in our day is not dissimilar.

I. Christian marriage in pagan society (vv. 10–11)
  A. The pagan approach to marriage
    1. A low view of women
    2. A preference for male company
    3. A reluctance to commit
    4. A casual attitude toward divorce
    5. A means of perpetuating a name
  B. The Christian view of marriage
    1. Originated as divine institution
    2. Perpetuated under divine instruction
      Note: "command"–a military term

    C. The Christian marriage in a pagan society
       1. It should offer something attractive
       2. It should function as corrective
       3. It should present an incentive

II. Mixed marriage in a pagan society (vv. 12–16)
    A. Believers married to willing unbelievers
       Note: "unbeliever" (Matt. 17:17; Acts 26:8; 2 Cor.
       6:14–16)
       1. Mixed marriage not grounds for divorce
          Note: initiative with the unbeliever
       2. Mixed marriage is grounds for "sanctification"
         a. "Sanctified" but not saved (1 Cor. 7:16)
         b. "Sanctified" but unbelieving (v. 14)
    B. Believers married to unwilling believers
       1. Believer must respond to unbeliever (v. 15)
       2. Believer must not be bound (v. 15)
       3. Believer must be at peace (v. 15)
       4. Believer must trust God (v. 16)

25

Calling, Culture, and Circumstance

1 Corinthians 7:17-24

To be called in the theological sense means two things—"to be invited" and "to be named," as in common usage. But the significance and ramifications of God's call to man are so important that they must be clearly understood.

I. The significance of "the calling"
   A. It is an invitation
      1. To enter God's kingdom (Matt. 22:9; 1 Thess. 2:12)
      2. To enjoy God's son (1 Cor. 1:9)
      3. To engage in God's service (Gal. 1:15)
   B. It is an identification
      1. The right to be called by his name (Acts 5:41; James 2:7)
      2. The right to call on his name (Gen. 4:26)

II. The substance of "the call"
   A. A call "of grace" (2 Tim. 1:9)
      1. Undeserved

       2. Unmerited
       3. Unappreciated
   B. A call "through gospel" (v. 10)
       1. The gospel portrayed
       2. The gospel preached
   C. A call "to glory" (Rom. 8:29–30)
       1. Glory begun (2 Cor. 3:18)
       2. Glory completed (Rom. 8:28)

III. The status of "the called"
   A. The called and their culture (1 Cor. 7:18–19)
     Note: the culture of "circumcised" and "uncir-
     cumcised" appreciated
       1. Culture appreciated in light of call
          a. Call is primary
          b. Culture is secondary
       2. Culture applied in light of commands
          a. Culture may be good
          b. Culture may be evil
          c. Culture may be neutral (v. 19)
   B. The called and their circumstances (vv. 21–22)
     Note: circumstances of "freeman" and "slave"
       1. The care-fulness that comes from "circum-
         stances"
          a. The shame of a slave
          b. The chance to be free
       2. The care-lessness that comes from "call"
          a. Called to be free though bound
          b. Called to be bound though free
            Note: the order must be call, circumstances,
            cares
   C. The called and their commitment
       1. Commitment to obey (v. 19)
       2. Commitment to abide (vv. 20, 24)

26

A Fresh Look at Marriage

1 Corinthians 7:25–40

Marriage has always been an opportunity for either heaven on earth or hell on earth. The Corinthians had some questions on the subject, and Paul's answers provide a different slant. His insights are mainly overlooked today.

I. Some prime considerations
   A. Spiritual considerations
      1. Receiving mercy from the Lord (v. 25)
      2. Caring for the things of the Lord (v. 32)
      3. Pleasing the Lord (v. 32)
      4. Attending to the Lord (v. 35)
      5. Only in the Lord (v. 39)
   B. Special considerations
      1. The present distress (v. 26)–marriage in the light of contemporary problems
      2. The time has been shortened (v. 29)–marriage in the light of eternal issues

    C. Social considerations
      1. The form of this world is passing away (v. 31)
      2. Marriage in the light of societal breakdowns
        (see 1 John 2:16–17)

 II. Some potential conflicts
    A. Conflicting pressures (1 Cor. 7:28)
      1. The pressure of multiplied responsibilities
      2. The pressure of divided resources
    B. Conflicting priorities (vv. 32–34)
      1. The priorities of time
      2. The priorities of involvement

III. Some practical conclusions
    A. The advantages of the single state
      1. Serving the Lord with dedication–holy (v. 34)
      2. Serving the Lord without distraction (v. 35)
      3. Serving the Lord with decisiveness (decreed)
        (v. 37)
    B. The adjustments in the marriage state–sacrificial
      adjustments
      1. To partners (v. 29)
      2. To problems (v. 30)
      3. To pleasures (v. 30)
      4. To possessions (v. 30)
      5. To privileges (v. 31)
    C. The attitudes to the widowed state (vv. 39–40)
      1. Freedom to remarry in the Lord
      2. Freedom to remain content in the Lord

27

Dealing with Controversy

1 Corinthians 8:1–13

In the ancient system of sacrifice only part of the sacrifice
was offered to the god. The balance was eaten either in
the temple or at home, sold in the marketplace, or given to
the poor. Eating meat offered to idols was, therefore, a matter that touched social, domestic, commercial, and moral
aspects as well as the spiritual. There was grave disagree-
ment among the Corinthians as to what they should do.
Paul handles the controversy.

  I. The differences that provoke controversy
     A. Differences in intellectual understanding (vv. 1, 7)
        1. Concerning the real nature of idols (v. 4)
        2. Concerning the unique being of God (v. 4)
        3. Concerning the reality of other powers (v. 5)
        4. Concerning the supremacy of Father and Son
           (v. 6)
     B. Differences in cultural background (v. 7)
        1. The importance of customs
        2. The impact of conscience

C. Differences in personal freedom (v. 9)
   1. Freedom to indulge
   2. Freedom not to indulge
D. Differences in spiritual maturity (vv. 10–11)
   1. Spiritual "weakness" producing scruples (v. 10)
   2. Spiritual "strength" producing stumbling blocks (v. 13)

II. The deficiencies that promote controversy
   A. Deficiencies of knowledge (v. 1)
      1. Not knowing the dangers of knowledge
      2. Not knowing the limitations of knowledge (v. 2)
   B. Deficiencies of love (v. 1)
      1. Love for God leading to being known (v. 3)
      2. Love for the weak leading to being kind (vv. 11–13)
   C. Deficiencies of perspective (v. 6)
      1. Our Father being the common source
      2. Our Lord being the common force
   D. Deficiencies of discipline (vv. 11–13)
      1. The discipline of personal freedom
      2. The discipline of "others" consciousness

III. The decisions that prohibit controversy
   A. Decisions concerning "puffing up" (v. 1)
   B. Decisions about "building up" (v. 1)
   C. Decisions about "tripping up" (v. 13)
   D. Decisions about "giving up" (v. 13)

28

Rights and the Christian

1 Corinthians 9:1-18

Freedom and rights are popular subjects. Most people are engaged in pursuing and enjoying them. But all is not well, and misunderstandings abound. The Christian has definite views on these matters that need to be both expressed and exemplified.

I. The contemporary attitude to the "rights" issue
   A. Development of the contemporary attitude
      1. Divine right of kings
      2. Magna Carta 1215
      3. Declaration of Independence 1776
      4. Bill of Rights 1791
      5. Universal Declaration of Human Rights 1948
      6. Civil Rights, Equal Rights Amendment, etc.
   B. Dangers of the contemporary attitude
      1. Danger of increased selfishness
      2. Danger of neglected responsibilities
      3. Danger of undeveloped initiatives

II. The Christian approach to the "rights" issue
  A. The recognition of human rights
      1. Inferred if not stated (see Exod. 20)
      2. Stated by Paul (1 Cor. 9)
          a. Right to be recognized (vv. 1–2)
          b. Right to be respected (vv. 3–5)
          c. Right to be rested (v. 6)
          d. Right to be rewarded (vv. 7–12)
  B. The repercussions of human rights
      1. Others may be offended (8:13)
      2. Gospel may be obstructed (9:12)
  C. The responsibilities of human rights
      1. Rights to be exercised to the glory of God
      2. Rights to be exercised to well-being of neighbor
      3. Rights to be exercised to spread of gospel
      4. Rights to be exercised to edifying of church
  D. The restraint of human rights
      1. Rights are secondary to responsibilities
      2. Rights are met when responsibilities are fulfilled
      3. Rights are subject to voluntary restraint

29

Christian Motivation

1 Corinthians 9:16-23

Motives are the thoughts and feelings that make people act. Motivation is the urge that directs people to accomplish goals they consider worthwhile. People are motivated by biological factors, desire for reward, fear of punishment, or high ideals and goals. The Christian desires to be motivated by the highest goals.

I. The origins of Christian motivation
   Note: "the law of Christ" (v. 21)
   A. The reality of the law of sin and death (Rom. 8:2)
   B. The release of the law of the spirit of life (v. 2)
   C. The ramifications of the law of God (v. 4)
      1. Loving through dependence (v. 5; Gal. 5:22)
      2. Loving by obedience (John 15:17; Rom. 13:8-10; Gal. 6:2)
   D. The repercussions of the law of Christ
      1. The Lord has laid necessity upon me (1 Cor. 9:16a)

Note: "necessity," literally "compulsion" (Matt. 14:22; Gal. 2:14)
2. The Lord has promised woe to me (1 Cor. 9:16b)
Note: "woe" can be denunciation (Matt. 23–24) or sorrow
3. The Lord has offered rewards to me (1 Cor. 9:17a)
   a. Immediately (v. 23)
   b. Ultimately (1 Cor. 3:14)
4. The Lord has committed stewardship to me (9:17b)
Note: "dispensation," literally "stewardship" (4:2)

II. The operation of Christian motivation
  A. It makes people more durable
     1. Suffering when they don't have to (9:12)
     2. Serving when they don't want to (v. 17)
  B. It makes people more expendable
     1. Saying no to a selfish role (v. 18)
     2. Saying yes to a serving role (v. 19)
  C. It makes people more flexible
     Note: "I became" (v. 20)
     1. In attitude–"all men" more important than prejudice
     2. In approach–"all means" justified by need
     3. In action–"all things" necessary to get job done

III. The outcome of Christian motivation
  A. An involvement in evangelization
     1. Gaining (vv. 19–22)
     2. Saving (v. 22)
  B. An enrichment in life (v. 23)–"partaking thereof"

30

Christian Service

1 Corinthians 9:24-27

Christians are "saved to serve." Their service is a result of their salvation, not vice versa. Service is an expression of gratitude and a token of concern that others should experience salvation. But not all the saved serve as they ought. Paul uses the Isthmian Games to illustrate his point.

I. The privilege of Christian service
   Note: "preach" (v. 27)—Greek *kerusso*, "to herald"
   A. The proclamation of an event (see 1 Tim. 2:7; 2 Tim. 1:1)
      1. The kingdom is at hand (Matt. 4:17–23)
      2. The jubilee has arrived (Luke 4:18–19; see Isa. 61:1)
      3. The resurrection is accomplished (1 Cor. 15:12)
   B. The call to worship
      1. The herald kept the peace
      2. The herald prepared the sacrifices
      3. The herald led the prayers

II. The pressures of Christian service
   A. The pressures of participation
      1. A race to be run (9:24)
         a. With a price (v. 24)
         b. With persistence (Gal. 5:7)
         c. With precision (1 Cor. 9:26, Gal. 2:2)
         d. With patience (Heb. 12:1)
      2. A fight to be fought (1 Cor. 9:25)
         Note: "strive" (v. 25)–Greek *agonizomai*, "to engage in"
         a. Wrestling in personal experience (Luke 13:24)
         b. Wrestling in prayerful concern (Col. 4:12)
         c. Wrestling in public involvement (1:28–29)
   B. The pressures of preparation
      1. The stripping down of the runner (Heb. 12:1)
      2. The strict discipline of the wrestler (1 Cor. 9:25)
      3. The self-denial of the boxer (v. 27)
   C. The pressures of penetration
      1. Running, not rambling (v. 26)
      2. Punching, not shadowboxing (v. 26)

III. The prize of Christian service
   Note: "crown"–Greek *stephanos*, "victor's wreath"
   A. A crown of rejoicing for the reproductive (1 Thess. 2:19)
   B. A crown of righteousness for the redeemed (2 Tim. 4:8)
   C. A crown of life for the resisters (James 1:12)
   D. A crown of glory for the responsible (1 Peter 5:4)

IV. Remember: the possibility of being disqualified (1 Cor. 9:27)

31

A Word of Warning

1 Corinthians 10:1-12

Both the Israelites in the wilderness and the Christians in Corinth misunderstood the way God operates, and therefore both had a false idea of their own situation. The Israelites were overthrown, and the Corinthians were warned the same thing could happen to them. We need to take heed of these things too.

I. The way God operates
  A. He formulates his plans
    1. To bring glory to himself
    2. To bring grace to the nations
  B. He equips his people
    1. By providing for them
      a. Deliverance (Exod. 14:13–31)
      b. Security (13:21)
      c. Leadership (14:31)
      d. Sustenance (16:4)
      e. Refreshment (17:6)

2. By proving them, he offers them opportunities to be
   a. Greedy or grateful (1 Cor. 10:6; see Ps. 78:17–19)
   b. Committed or compromised (1 Cor. 10:7; see Exod. 32:1–6)
   c. Disciplined or dissolute (1 Cor. 10:8; see Num. 25:1–2)
   d. Faithful or faithless (1 Cor. 10:9; see Exod. 17:2, 7)
   e. Content or contentious (1 Cor. 10:10; see Num. 14:2; 16:41)
3. By pruning them (see John 15:2; Heb. 12:3–15)
   a. He removes candlesticks (e.g., Rev. 2:5)
   b. He replaces kings (e.g., 1 Sam. 15:26–28)
   c. He rejects generations (e.g., Deut. 1:35–38)
C. He fulfills his purposes
   1. Nothing and nobody will stop him
   2. He will alter the means to achieve his ends
   3. The wise person does things his way

II. The warning God offers—take heed to:
   A. Think clearly
   B. Evaluate carefully
   C. Act consistently

32

Temptation

1 Corinthians 10:12-15

Temptation is a universal human problem. It is "common to men." Nevertheless, it is not universally understood. Sometimes "temptation" in the Bible means "solicitation to do evil," but other times it means "testing." But always temptation comes under the ultimate control of the faithful God who can bring blessing out of every temptation. Still, human cooperation is necessary.

I. The universal problem
  A. The malevolent forces
    1. Satan committed to destroy
      a. Humanity (Gen. 3)
      b. Christ (Luke 4)
      c. Church (1 Peter 5:8)
      d. Individuals (Luke 22:31)
    2. Society corrupted by godlessness (1 John 2:15–17)
    3. Self confounded by selfishness (James 1:14)

    B. The neutral force—natural laws that can bless or blight (e.g., gravity)

    C. The benevolent force—God who is committed to developing us

       1. By planning tests producing obedience and dependence (e.g., Gen. 22; Exod. 16; Deut. 13)

       2. By permitting temptations and offering alternatives

         a. Being seduced or strengthened

         b. Experiencing God's power or own weakness

         c. Going wrong or doing right

         d. Suffering disaster or making discoveries

    D. The practical factors

       1. Testing through societal problems

       2. Testing through physical pain

       3. Testing through natural personality

       4. Testing through financial pressures

 II. God's unequivocal promises

    A. To limit the pressure

    B. To provide the safety valve

    C. To encourage endurance

III. The undeniable prospects

    A. Spiritual development

       1. Through obedience

         a. Taking heed (1 Cor. 10:12)

         b. Taking flight (v. 14)

         c. Taking issue (1 Peter 5:9)

       2. Through dependence on the faithfulness of God

    B. Spiritual disaster

       1. Through disobedience

       2. Through independence

33

Religious Observances

1 Corinthians 10:16-22

Religion is an enormous factor in the human race. Edmund Burke called man "a religious animal." Marx said religion was "the opium of the people." Freud called it "an illusion." Paul showed how Christian, Jew, and pagan all have religious convictions and practices. He offered sound words of instruction and warning concerning the use or abuse of religious activity.

I. The rites that are part of religion
   A. The Jewish sacrificial system (v. 18)
   B. The pagan idolatrous sacrifices (v. 20)
   C. The Christian communion service (v. 16)
      1. The cup we bless
      2. The bread we break

II. The realities that are part of the rites
   A. The reality of spiritual presence
      1. Behind the altar stands God (v. 20)
      2. Behind the idol stands the demon (v. 20)
      3. Behind the communion stands the Lord (v. 21)

B. The reality of spiritual participation
   Note: "communion" (v. 16), "partakers" (v. 18), "fellowship" (v. 20) from Greek *koin*
   1. Participation in benefits of sacrifice (v. 18)
   2. Participation in activities of demons (v. 20)
   3. Participation in relationship with Christ (v. 16)
      a. Relationship of forgiveness through the bread
      b. Relationship of wholeness through the bread
      c. Relationship of togetherness through the body (v. 17)

III. The repercussions that are part of the realities
   A. The necessity of promoting the body (v. 17)
   B. The possibility of provoking the Lord (v. 22)
   C. The necessity of proscribing the demonic (v. 21)

34

Knowing What to Do

1 Corinthians 10:23–11:1

Life is full of perplexities and decisions. Many decisions come easily because definite rules are spelled out. Things are much less simple when rules are not clearly laid down, especially in the area of personal relationships.

    I. Factors that must be understood
       A. Personal factors
          1. Personal freedom (v. 23)
          2. Personal development
             Note: "expedient," "edify" (v. 23)
          3. Personal enjoyment (vv. 25, 30)
          4. Personal wholeness (v. 26)
          5. Personal convictions (v. 27)
       B. Social factors
          1. Social possibilities
             a. The marketplace (v. 25)
             b. The holy place (v. 28)
             c. The meeting place (v. 27)

        2. Social problems

           a. Differences stemming from conscience (vv. 28–29)

           b. Differences related to culture (v. 32)

           Note: Jews, Gentiles, church of God

    C. Spiritual factors

        1. God must be glorified (v. 31)

           a. By what is done

           b. By the way it is done

        2. People must be saved (v. 33)

           a. Alternatives must be portrayed

           b. Opportunities must be presented

II. Actions that must be undertaken

    A. Actions that demonstrate freedom (vv. 25–27)

    B. Actions that display flexibility

        1. With regard to welfare of others (v. 24)

        2. With regard to scruples of others (v. 29)

        Note: restrain your liberty rather than have it destroyed

        3. With regard to the offense of others (v. 32)

        4. With regard to the salvation of others (v. 33)

    C. Actions that denote "following" (11:1)

    Note: "followers," literally "imitators"

        1. Imitate God-given leadership

        2. Emulate Spirit-given lordship

35

Women in the Church

1 Corinthians 11:2-16

Some people say that Christianity has kept women in a degraded position, while others insist that it has exalted the status of women to unknown heights. Paul's view of women as expressed to the Corinthians has been the subject of much debate. Let's join it!

I. The situation in the Corinthian church
   A. Cultural variations
      1. Jewish
      2. Roman
      3. Corinthian
   B. Controversial veils
      1. Some men were wearing veils to pray
      2. Some women were not
   C. Conflicting views
      1. Wearing veils showed reverence
      2. Not wearing veils showed liberty

II. The statement to the Corinthian church
Note: difficulties of interpretation
A. Hierarchical interpretation
1. God is superior to Christ
2. Christ is superior to man
3. Man is superior to woman
4. Unveiled man shows his superiority
5. Veiled woman shows her subjugation
6. Women must veil because of angels
B. Egalitarian interpretation
1. In Christ there is equality (v. 11)
2. Head means source of life
3. Veiled men dishonor Christ
4. Unveiled women may dishonor husband because of culture
5. Men in the image of God need no veil
6. Women equal with men need not veil
7. Women have "power" to choose
8. Woman's hair is her veil
9. Don't argue about it

III. The significance for the contemporary church
A. Hierarchical view
1. Man is superior and woman is subservient
2. Man must speak and woman must be silent
B. Egalitarian view
1. Women should be viewed as people
2. In Christ there is equality
3. Church must provide for emancipated women

36

Church Life

1 Corinthians 11:17-22

hristians have a personal relationship with Christ that affects every aspect of their lives. They also have a relationship to other believers that is lived out in the context of the church. Because of its unique role, the church needs to ensure that Christians are aware of the importance of "church life."

I. The unique design of the church
   A. A "called-out" community
      Note: "church" (vv. 18, 22)—Greek *ekklesia,* literally "called out"
      1. Hebrew idea—theocracy (see Acts 7:38), a society called by God to himself
      2. Greek idea—democracy (19:32, 39, 41), a society free to govern its affairs
      3. Christian idea—theocratic democracy, a free society governed by God

B. A "come together" community (1 Cor. 11:17–18, 20, 33, 34)
  1. The president of the community–Christ the Lord
  2. The purpose of the community–service
  3. The power of the community–love
  4. The principles of the community–faith and obedience

II. The ugly discrepancies in the church
  A. Becoming worse instead of better (v. 17)
  B. Becoming divided instead of devoted (v. 18)
  C. Becoming worldly instead of worshipful (vv. 20–21)
  D. Becoming selfish instead of serving (v. 22)

III. The unavoidable directions to the church
  A. A matter of authority
     Note: "declare" (v. 17), literally "instruct"
  B. A matter of attitude
     1. Don't believe all you hear (v. 18)
     2. Do see the value in negative things (v. 19)
  C. A matter of action
     1. Accept the rebuke
     2. Admit the truth
     3. Act accordingly–"set in order" (v. 34)

37

What to Do at the Communion

1 Corinthians 11:23-33

Christians know that the Lord instituted the communion service on the night of his betrayal and that he expects them to participate regularly in this act of worship. The church has traditionally perpetuated this observance, but individuals have not always known what to do at the communion. Here is some advice Paul gave the Corinthians.

    I. Take an upward look—"I received of the Lord . . ." (v. 23)
       A. The communion has divine origins
       B. The communion has divine authority—"this do"
       C. The communion has divine significance
          Note: the communion an antidote to secularism

   II. Take a backward look—"the night in which he was betrayed" (v. 23)
       A. The events of the evening
       B. The explanation of the events
          1. The explanation of the foot washing

  2. The explanation of the broken bread
  3. The explanation of the cup
   Note: the communion an antidote to forget-
   fulness

III. Take a forward look—"till he comes" (v. 26)
 A. The temporary nature of the communion
 B. The certain promise of the return
  Note: the communion an antidote to carelessness

IV. Take an inward look—"let a man examine himself"
 (v. 28)
 A. The reality of personal recollection (v. 24)
 B. The necessity of personal declaration (v. 26)
 C. The necessity of personal appreciation (vv. 24–25)
 D. The necessity of personal evaluation (v. 28)

V. Take an outward look—"tarry one for another" (v. 33)
 A. The readiness to see each other
  1. Weak
  2. Sickly
  3. Hungry
  4. Drunken
 B. The willingness to serve each other

38

Concerning Spiritual Gifts I

1 Corinthians 12:1-11

One of the ministries of the Holy Spirit is to dispense "gifts" to believers. He had done this in superlative fashion in Corinth. But both those of Hebrew and Greek background had understood these gifts more in terms of culture than Christ, so chaos had resulted. Paul endeavors to clarify the situation.

I. The Corinthians' abuse of spiritual gifts
   A. The excesses of Greek paganism
      Note: "carried away" (v. 2), possible demonism
   B. The extremes of Hebrew holy men (e.g., Ezekiel, David, Samson, Isaiah)
   C. The experience of the Corinthian church
      1. Attracted to the unusual (vv. 8–10)
      2. Indulging in the irrational and ecstatic
      3. Flirting with the blasphemous (v. 3)

II. The Christian attitude toward spiritual gifts
   A. Recognize the place of spiritual gifts
      1. The Holy Spirit is the Gift

    2. The Holy Spirit gives the gifts
      a. To each Christian (v. 7)
      b. To profit the body (v. 7)
      c. As he chooses (v. 11)
      d. With great variety (v. 4)
      e. For different ministries (v. 5)
      f. In various operations (v. 6)
B. Recognize the purposes of spiritual gifts–to build up the body of believers by:
    1. Enlisting
    2. Enriching
    3. Enabling
    4. Encouraging
C. Recognize the plethora of spiritual gifts
    1. The Corinthian lists (vv. 8–10, 28)
    2. The Roman list (Rom. 12:6–8)
    3. The Ephesian list (Eph. 4:7–11)
D. Recognize the privilege of spiritual gifts
    1. How to identify gifts
    2. How to exercise gifts
E. Recognize the problems of spiritual gifts–the possibilities of being:
    1. Unappreciated
    2. Undiscovered
    3. Unused
    4. Unbalanced
    5. Uncontrolled
F. Recognize the potential of spiritual gifts when exercised:
    1. In love (1 Cor. 13)
    2. In the Spirit
    3. With enthusiasm (Rom. 12:7)

39

Concerning Spiritual Gifts II

1 Corinthians 12:1-11

I. The use of spiritual gifts
  A. Gifts require correct evaluation
    1. Given by the Spirit (v. 4)
    2. For ministries of the Lord (v. 4)
  B. Gifts require careful identification
    1. Specific gifts for church office (v. 28; also Rom. 12; Eph. 4)
      a. Apostles—purifiers of doctrine, pioneers
      b. Prophets—forthtellers, foretellers of truth
      c. Teachers—instructors
      d. Evangelists—traveling presenters of evangel
      e. Pastors—overseers of congregation
      f. Rulers—those who "stand before"
    2. Special gifts for Christian ministry
      a. Word of wisdom—ability to explain "wisdom of God" (1 Cor. 12:1)
      b. Word of knowledge—ability to know what you didn't know you knew

   c. Faith–ability to believe God when others
      are floundering
   d. Healing–ability to convey God's sovereign
      healing ability
   e. Miracles–ability to be involved in God
      doing the unusual
   f. Prophecy–see "Prophets" above
   g. Discerner of spirits–ability to evaluate spir-
      itual profession and ministry
   h. Tongues–ability to speak in unknown lan-
      guages
   i. Interpretation–ability to interpret tongues
   j. Exhortation–ability to encourage
   k. Helpers–ability to be supportive
   l. Acts of mercy–ability to serve and be cheer-
      ful about it
   m. Many others
   C. Gifts require constant application (see Rom.
      12:6–8; 2 Tim. 1:6)

 II. The disuse of spiritual gifts
   A. Some gifts may no longer be applicable
   B. Some people may not know about their gifts
   C. Some may refuse to exercise what they have

III. The abuse of spiritual gifts
   A. Exercising of gift for wrong motive
   B. Making gifts cause of disunity rather than means
      of unity

IV. The misuse of spiritual gifts
   A. "Teaching" without the truth
   B. "Prophesying" without the Spirit
   C. "Leading" without direction
   D. "Healing" without God's blessing
   E. "Speaking in tongues" without love

40

The Baptism of the Spirit

1 Corinthians 12:12–14

The baptism of the Spirit was predicted by John the Baptist (Mark 1:8), promised by the Lord Jesus (Acts 1:5), experienced by the disciples (Acts 11:15–17), and taught by Paul (1 Cor. 12:13). But today the subject is clouded by controversy.

I. The "charismatic" view of the baptism
   A. Outline of this view
      1. The Spirit works in conviction and regeneration
      2. He works in baptism
      3. The baptism equips for a life of power and service
      4. The baptism is confirmed by "glossalalia"
      5. Believers should seek this baptism
   B. Origins of this view
      1. The disciples at Pentecost (Acts 2)
      2. The converts at Samaria (Acts 8)
      3. The conversion of Paul (Acts 9)

4. The conversion of Cornelius (Acts 10)
5. The disciples at Ephesus (Acts 19)
C. Objections to this view
1. Personal experiences regarded as normative
2. Transitional period regarded as permanent
3. Didactic element entirely missing
4. Contradicted by other Scriptures
5. Differing terms regarded as synonymous

II. The "traditional" view of the baptism
A. Outline of this view
1. John's baptism introduced Christ's kingdom
2. Spirit's baptism initiated Christ's body
3. All believers in the body
4. All believers are partakers of the Spirit
B. Origins of this view
1. Scriptures on the subject rare
2. Relate to John's prediction of Pentecost
3. "Filling" of the Spirit and baptism—synchronous, not synonymous
4. Paul addresses "all" Corinthian believers
5. Baptism not sign of spirituality
6. Nowhere linked with tongues
7. Never told to seek it
C. Objections to this view
1. Experience of the early disciples
2. Experience of contemporary people

III. Suggested conclusions
A. Let's rejoice that the Holy Spirit is given to all believers
B. Let's admit that no one has exhausted his capabilities
C. Let's allow him to work as he chooses
D. Let's be eager to search the Scriptures and follow through

41

Gifts and the Body

1 Corinthians 12:12–31

I. The design of the body
  A. Designed to provide the means of Christ's activity
     Note: a physical body allows a spiritual entity to
     function in a physical environment
     1. Christ's role (vv. 12, 27)
        a. The body is the body of Christ
        b. The members are the members of Christ
     2. The Spirit's role (v. 13)
        a. The members baptized by the Spirit
        b. The members "watered" by the Spirit
     3. The Father's role
        a. The Father "chooses" the place (v. 18)
        b. The Father "tempers" the body (v. 24)
        c. The Father "sets" the members (v. 28)

B. Designed to promote the measure of its own health

Note: like the human body, the body of Christ has the means of preserving its own health

1. Homeostasis—"maintenance of internal environment"
2. Adaptation—"adjustment to severe stress"
3. Defense against biotic invasion
   a. The inflammatory response
   b. The immune response
4. Repair of damaged cells
5. Hemostatis—sealing of vessels to stop loss of blood

II. The defects of the body
 A. Caused by environment or heredity; e.g., Jew, Greek, slave, freeman (v. 13)
 B. Caused by injury to member; e.g., hurt member no longer part of body (vv. 15–16)
 C. Caused by abnormal growth of cells; e.g., the whole body an eye (v. 17)
 D. Caused by psychological problems; e.g., aggression (v. 21), shame (vv. 22–24)
 E. Caused by nutritional deficiency or excess; e.g., members not "caring" (v. 25)
 F. Caused by immune hyper-reaction; e.g., schism in the body (v. 25)

III. The desire of the body—the best gifts for the good of the body

42

Spiritual Gifts and Love

1 Corinthians 13:1-4

Spiritual gifts exercised without love become nonproductive and even counterproductive. Paul found it necessary to explain this to the Corinthians. But the problem then and now is how to explain love and how to express it.

I. Love explained
  A. Some contemporary concepts
    1. Love is sentimental—falling in love
    2. Love is sexual—making love
    3. Love is situational—only the command to love is categorically good
  B. Some biblical perspectives
    1. Love is revealed in the divine nature—"God is love" (1 John 4:16)
       Note: all we know of God is an expression of love
    2. Love is revealed in the divine behavior—"I will love them freely" (Hos. 11:1-4; 14:1-9)
    3. Love is revealed in the divine demands—"Thou shalt love . . . " (Matt. 22:36-40)

      4. Love is revealed in the divine relationships—
"my beloved Son" (Luke 3:22)
Note: Romans 8:32

      5. Love is revealed in the divine initiatives—"God so loved that he gave" (John 3:16)

      6. Love is revealed in the divine incarnation—
"Herein is love . . ." (1 John 4:10)

II. Love experienced

  A. The experience of "eros" love (egotistic—desire to get, not give)

  B. The experience of "philea" love (mutualistic—desire to give and get)

  C. The experience of "agape" love (altruistic—desire to give without getting)

      1. Being conscious of this love (Rom. 5:8)

      2. Being conquered by this love (Gal. 2:20)

      3. Being confident in this love (Rom. 8:37–39)
Note: agape love desires and does the good of the beloved

III. Love expressed

  A. Agape love is the Christian distinctive (John 13:35; Gal. 5:6)

      1. Expressed to God

        a. Desires his good

        b. Incorporates trust and obedience

      2. Expressed to self

        a. Desires own good for God's sake

        b. Loving oneself selflessly (Kierkegaard)

      3. Expressed to neighbor

        a. Brother/neighbor—"as I loved you" (John 15:12)

        b. Enemy/neighbor (Matt. 5:44; Rom. 5:10)

  B. Agape love is the Christian imperative

      1. Love is something you do

      2. Love is fruit of Spirit (Gal. 5:22)

43

Love Is...

1 Corinthians 13:4-7

It's not hard to talk about love or sing about it. Doing it is the problem!

I. The dimensions of love
   A. Love—the essence of God's being (1 John 4:16)
   B. Love—the epitome of divine demands (Matt. 22:38–40)
   C. Love—the evidence of saving faith (1 John 4:20–21)
   D. Love—the effect of Spirit's activity (Gal. 5:22)
   E. Love—the expression of Christian uniqueness (John 13:35)

II. The description of love
   A. Love is long-suffering—Greek, literally "long wrathed" (e.g., Heb. 6:15; 2 Peter 3:9)
   B. Love is kind—Greek, also translated "gentleness," "goodness" (e.g., Matt. 11:30; Rom. 2:4; Gal. 5:22)

  C. Love is not envious—Greek, also translated "zealous" (e.g., James 4:2, "the desire to have")

  D. Love is not boastful (only use in New Testament)

  E. Love is not proud (see 1 Cor. 13:4, 6; 5:2; 8:1)

  F. Love is well-behaved—ethical standards (e.g., Mark 15:43; Rom. 1:27; 1 Cor. 7:36; 14:20)

  G. Love is not insistent on its own way (e.g., 10:24, 33; Phil. 2:21)

  H. Love is not provoked—Greek, literally "sharpened," "needled" (e.g., Acts 15:39; 17:16)

  I. Love is not "calculating" evil; e.g., attributing evil motive, keeping accounts

  J. Love is not glad about evil; e.g., enjoying someone's discomfort, downfall

  K. Love is thrilled with truth; e.g., has fine sense of moral rectitude

  L. Love is durable—Greek, literally "to protect by covering watertight"

  M. Love is trusting; e.g., retains faith in, believes best about

  N. Love is optimistic; e.g., refuses to believe failure is final

  O. Love is tenacious—Greek, literally "abides under" (e.g., Heb. 12:2)

  P. Love is eternally relevant—Greek, literally "never fails" (e.g., Luke 16:17)

III. The dynamics of love

  A. The dynamic of a renewed mind—seeing man as God sees

  B. The dynamic of a regenerated spirit—the Holy Spirit at work

  C. The dynamic of a renewed will—a will willing what God wills

44

Love Is #1

1 Corinthians 13:8-13

With the emphasis on the gifts of the Spirit in Corinth there had been a corresponding underemphasis on love, and considerable strife had resulted. Paul carefully pointed out the superiority of love to all the gifts.

I. Love is superior to the gifts
   A. Because of the limitations of gifts
      1. Gifts will be terminated (v. 8)
         a. End of apostolic era?
         b. Completion of canon of Scripture?
         c. When Christ returns?
         d. At different times? (cf. vv. 8 and 9)
      2. Gifts can be overrated (v. 9)
         a. Gifts are less than the revelation ("part")
         b. Gifts are limited by the recipients
         c. Love will outlast and outshine gifts
   B. Because of the intimations of glory
      1. Glory means total completion (v. 10)
         Note: "that which is perfect"–Greek *to teleion*

2. Glory means total comprehension (v. 11), literally "no longer talking, feeling, reasoning like a baby"
3. Glory means total communication (v. 12a), literally "no longer looking in enigmatic mirror"
4. Glory means total communion (v. 12b)
   Note: cf. *ginosko* = know (first usage), *epiginosko* = know fully (second, third usage)
5. Glory will stimulate love, not gifts

II. Love is supreme among the graces
    Note: cf. Greek "graces," brightness, joyfulness, bloom
    A. The graces are indispensable
       1. Destruction is the alternative to faith
       2. Despair is the alternative to hope
       3. Disintegration is the alternative to love
    B. The graces are interrelated
       1. Faith is the root of human experience
       2. Hope is the branch of faith
       3. Love is the fruit of faith and hope
    C. But love's supremacy is indisputable
       1. Because of its intrinsic excellence
          Note: God is love, not faith or hope
       2. Because of its unselfish nature
          Note: faith and hope have selfish implications
       3. Because of eternal significance
          Note: eternity will diminish the need for faith and hope but will develop capacity for love

45

Make Love Your Aim

1 Corinthians 14:1

Businessmen are taught "management by objectives." Athletes are coached on the basis of a "game plan," and many other people are exhorted to set for themselves "goals to live by." Christians are told "follow after love," which translated literally means "set love as your goal and go for it." But how can we do this?

I. By embracing spiritual truths
   A. The necessity of spiritual goals
      1. Goal of edification (Rom. 14:19)
      2. Goal of hospitality (12:13)
      3. Goal of goodness (1 Thess. 5:15)
      4. Goal of godliness (1 Tim. 6:11)
      5. Goal of holiness (Heb. 12:14)
         Note: Paul's statement (Phil. 3:12–14)
   B. The supremacy of love (John 13:35)
      1. Supreme because of divine qualities (1 John 4:16)

    2. Supreme because of unique qualities (1 Cor. 13:4–7)

    3. Supreme because of abiding qualities (v. 8)

    4. Supreme because of eternal qualities (v. 13)

  C. The supreme necessity of love as goal

II. By employing special factors

  A. The factor of the Scriptures (Rom. 15:1–4)

  B. The factor of prayer (Luke 6:28)

  C. The factor of the Spirit (Gal. 5:22–23)

  D. The factor of lordship (Luke 6:46)

III. By embarking on specific actions

  A. In the area of existing relationships

    1. Evaluation

      a. How do I see them?

      b. How do they see me?

    2. Reconciliation

      a. Be prepared to take initiative

      b. Be willing to be rejected

    3. Consolidation

      a. Take positive steps to build relationship

      b. Take positive action to build up people

  B. In the area of expanding relationships

    1. A matter of insight

      a. See people in the divine perspective

      b. Love people because of divine directive

    2. A matter of involvement

      a. The involvement of your time

      b. The investment of yourself

      c. The integration of your lifestyle

46

Make Ministry Your Emphasis

1 Corinthians 14:1-12

Having taught the Corinthians to "make love their aim," Paul went on to say that they should concentrate on ministering to each other instead of emphasizing the gifts that would minister to themselves.

I. Carefully establish spiritual goals
   A. Make love your general aim
   B. Make edification of the church your specific aim (vv. 4–5, 12)
      1. By insight into the nature of the church
      2. By involvement in the growth of the church
      3. By investment in the life of the church

II. Correctly emphasize spiritual gifts
   A. The place of spiritual gifts
      1. Given by the Spirit
      2. Given to the people
      3. Given for the church
         Note: Corinthians were "zealots" when it came to gifts (v. 12; also 12:31; 14:1, 39)

B. The priorities of spiritual gifts
   1. The value of speaking in tongues
      a. Speaking to God (v. 2)
      b. Mysteries in the Spirit (v. 2)
      c. Self-edification (v. 4)
      d. With interpretation, church edification (v. 5)
      e. Paul encourages it to a degree (v. 5)
   2. The limitation of speaking in tongues
      a. Lack of edification (vv. 6–11)
      b. Lack of communication
   3. The value of prophetic ministries
      a. Speaks to men (v. 3)
      b. Edifies the church (v. 4)
      c. Instructs the mind (v. 7)
      d. Prepares for battle (v. 8)
C. Prophecy as a spiritual gift
   1. In the historic sense
      a. A ministry of instruction; e.g., Moses (Deut. 6)
      b. A ministry of correction; e.g., Jeremiah (Jer. 7)
      c. A ministry of persuasion; e.g., Jonah (Jonah 3)
      d. A ministry of prediction; e.g., Daniel
   2. In the contemporary sense
      Note: possible change in 2 Peter 2:1
      a. A ministry of prophesying, literally "speak forth" (1 Cor. 14:3)
      b. A ministry of edifying, literally "building a house"
      c. A ministry of encouraging, literally "calling alongside"
      d. A ministry of consoling, literally "speaking closely"
      e. A ministry of revealing, literally "unveiling" (v. 6)
      f. A ministry of knowing
      g. A ministry of teaching
      h. A ministry of profiting

47

Minds Matter Immensely

1 Corinthians 14:13-25

When love is the prevailing attitude and ministry the major activity, the church will be edified, provided the people's minds are maturing in the things of God.

I. The functions of the mind
   A. The mind is a computer (John 8:32)
   B. The mind is a coach (13:17)
   C. The mind is a critic (Rom. 7:23–25)

II. The failures of the mind
   A. The unregenerate mind
      1. Dishonest (1:28)
      2. Vain (Eph. 4:17)
      3. Corrupt (1 Tim. 6:5)
      4. Defiled (Titus 1:15)
   B. The unfruitful mind (1 Cor. 14:14–15)
      1. Inspiration without information
      2. Information without inspiration

   C. The undeveloped mind (v. 20)
     1. Little information
     2. Little integration
     3. Little inspiration
   D. The unstable mind (2 Thess. 2:2)
     1. Lacking in discernment
     2. Lacking in conviction
   E. The unhealthy mind (Col. 2:18)
     1. Short on humility
     2. Short on balance
       Note: Philippians 4:7

III. The fitness of the mind (1 Cor. 14:20)
   A. The factors of this fitness
     1. An opened mind (Luke 24:45)
       Note: *understand,* literally "put together"
     2. A renewed mind (Rom. 12:2)
     3. An enriched mind (1 Cor. 2:16)
     4. An integrated mind (1:10)
     5. A convinced mind (Rom. 14:5)
   B. The fruits of this fitness
     1. Relating to God (1 Cor. 14:15)
     2. Relating to the church (vv. 16–19)
     3. Relating to people (v. 20b)
     4. Relating to unbelievers (vv. 21–25)

48

Togetherness

1 Corinthians 14:26–40

Including the section of the epistle dealing with the gifts of the Spirit and the operation in the church, Paul stresses the need for "coming together" and gives practical direction designed to promote and preserve "togetherness."

I. The objectives of togetherness must be recognized
   A. General togetherness in human society
      1. The safety of balanced opinions (Prov. 11:14)
      2. The security of shared responsibility (Eccles. 4:9–12)
      3. The stimulation of united activity (Lev. 26:8)
   B. Special togetherness in the Christian church
      1. The framework "in my name" (Matt. 18:20)
      2. The focus "in the midst" (v. 20)
      3. The function
         a. Sharing together (Acts 2:44)
         b. Praying together (4:31; 12:12)
         c. Problem solving together (15:6)
         d. Communing together (20:7)

       e. Ministering together (Phil. 1:27)
       f. Growing together (Col. 2:2)
       g. Learning together (1 Cor. 14:26)

  II. The obstacles to togetherness must be removed
    A. Attitudes that are obstacles
      1. Nonparticipation (Heb. 10:24–25)
      2. Nonacceptance (James 2:1–2)
    B. Actions that are obstacles
      1. In matters of discipline
        a. Individualism (1 Cor. 14:26–29)
        b. Lack of restraint (vv. 34–35)
          (1) The cultural theory
          (2) The charismatic theory
          (3) The chattering theory
        c. Lack of respect (vv. 36–38)
      2. In matters of discernment (vv. 30–33)

 III. The opportunities for togetherness must be redeemed
    A. By developing a sense of community
    B. By developing an attitude of commitment
    C. By developing a sense of contribution (v. 26)

49

The Gospel

1 Corinthians 15:1-8

Some of the Corinthians were having doubts about whether dead people could be raised. As the Christian gospel hinges on the resurrection of Christ, Paul saw the seriousness of their questioning. So he gave a refresher course on the gospel.

I. The concept of the gospel
   A. The Hebrew concept
      1. The proclaiming of good news
      2. Victory (Isa. 52:7)
   B. The Greek concept
      1. Similar to above, including reward for good news
      2. Romans used term to announce birth, coming of age, accession of emperor
   C. The Christian concept
      1. The proclamation of God's kingdom (Matt. 4:23)
      2. The promise of God's intervention (Luke 4:18)
      3. The power of God's activity (Rom. 1:16)

II. The content of the gospel
    A. The problem of sin
        1. Its character
            a. Transgression–doing what is forbidden
            b. Sin–not doing what is required
            c. Iniquity–perfecting what is false
        2. Its consequences
            a. A barrier to God's presence
            b. A blight on human experience
    B. The person of Christ
        1. His activity
            a. He was crucified
            b. He was buried
            c. He was raised
            d. He was recognized (1 Cor. 15:5–8)
        2. His credibility
            a. Theologically respectable–"according to the Scriptures" (vv. 3–4)
            b. Historically verifiable

III. The consequences of the gospel
    A. Having been revealed it must be relayed (v. 3)
        1. Preaching
        2. Delivering
    B. Having been relayed it must be received (v. 1)
        1. In which you stand
        2. By which you are being saved (v. 2)
    C. Having been received it must be retained
        1. Holding firmly to . . .
        2. . . . believing in vain

50

The Grace of God

1 Corinthians 15:8-11

The grace of God was so dominant in Paul's thinking that he began and ended every epistle by referring to it. Much of the effectiveness of his life and ministry is directly attributable to his understanding of the working of God's grace in his life.

> O to grace how great a debtor
> Daily I'm constrained to be
> Let that grace now, like a fetter
> Bind my wandering heart to Thee.

I. The grace of God—a divine attitude (vv. 8–10a)
  A. The problem of divine-human relations
    1. The moral failure of humanity
    2. The absolute justice of God
    3. The spiritual importance of mankind
    4. The total independence of God
  B. The power of divine intervention
    1. Called by grace (Gal. 1:15)

    2. Justified by grace (Rom. 3:21ff.)
    3. Enriched by grace (Eph. 1:7)
       Note: "By the grace of God I am what I am"

II. The grace of God—a dynamic stimulus
  A. The misunderstanding of grace
    1. The abuse of grace (Rom. 6:1)
    2. The ignorance of salvation
  B. The application of grace
    1. A life of gratitude (1 Cor. 15:10b)
    2. A life of graciousness (Col. 4:6)
    3. A life of growth (2 Tim. 2:1ff.)
       Note: "His grace was bestowed . . . not in vain"

III. The grace of God—a daily enabling
  A. God's equipment for God's requirement
    1. Demonstrated in Christ (John 1:14)
    2. Distributed by the Spirit (v. 16)
      a. The gift of the Spirit
      b. The gifts of the Spirit
        Note: *charismata* (1 Cor. 12), *pneumatika* (1 Cor. 14)
        Note: "The grace of God that was with me . . ." (15:10)

51

The Resurrection of Christ

1 Corinthians 15:12-19

A segment of the Corinthian church was denying the possibility of men rising from the dead. But the Christian gospel insists that Christ rose from the dead. The contradiction had to be resolved in Corinth, for as Paul shows, if Christ is not risen, Christianity is nonsense.

I. The proclamation of the Christian gospel
   "Christ was raised from the dead . . ." (v. 12)
   A. Historical evidence
      1. An empty tomb
      2. Numerous appearances
      3. Transformed lives
   B. Theological explanation
      1. Christ rose bodily from the grave
      2. God did it
         a. To fulfill his divine purposes
         b. To demonstrate his divine power
         c. To authenticate his divine promises

II. The objections to the Christian proclamation
    A. Dead men don't rise again (a denial of possibility of divine intervention)
    B. So Christ could not have risen
    C. Alternative explanations must be found
       1. The Fraud theory
       2. The Swoon theory
       3. The Delusion theory

III. The implications of these objections
    A. Christian message is untrue (v. 14a)
    B. Christian faith is without validity (v. 14b)
    C. Christian witness is misrepresenting God (v. 15)
    D. Christian "forgiveness" is a fallacy (v. 17)
    E. Christian burial is a hoax (v. 18)
    F. Christian hope is futile (v. 19)

IV. The challenge to the Christian church
    A. Christ is risen
       1. So Christianity is vital, irrepressible, and powerful
       2. So Christians are hopeful and fearless
    B. Christ is not risen
       1. So Christianity is nonsense
       2. So the church is a phony

52

God's Agenda

1 Corinthians 15:20-28

Having shown the inevitable results of denying the resurrection of the dead in general and Christ in particular, Paul goes on to show that Christ's resurrection is a basic part of God's agenda for the future.

I. The resurrection of Christ
   A. Its statement (v. 20a)
      1. Evidence of divine intervention
      2. Basis of human assurance
   B. Its significance (vv. 20b–22)
      1. The firstfruits of God's harvest (see Lev. 23:10)
         a. Christ the firstfruits (not the first) from the dead
         b. Firstfruits consecrate the latter fruits
         c. Firstfruits assume later fruit
      2. The antidote to Adam's disease (see Rom. 5:12–19)
         a. Adam's sin produced death
         b. "In Adam" disease is contagious, infectious, and epidemic
         c. Christ's resurrection produced life
         d. "In Christ" healing is available

C. Its structure (1 Cor. 15:23)
   1. First, the firstfruits
   2. Second, the dead in Christ (1 Thess. 4:16)
   3. Third, those alive and remaining

II. The return of Christ (1 Cor. 15:23b)
    Note: "his coming"–Greek *parousia*
    A. The promise of his return (see John 14:3; Acts 1:11)
       1. Personally
       2. Suddenly
       3. Definitely
       4. Triumphantly
    B. The purpose of his coming
       1. To gather the redeemed (Matt. 24:31)
       2. To judge the world (25:32–46)
       3. To raise the dead (1 Thess. 4:13–18)

III. The reign of Christ
     Note: "the end"–Greek *telos,* literally the "climax" or "consummation"
     A. The overpowering of all powers (1 Cor. 15:24)
        1. Death will be the last enemy to be defeated
        2. Death will be the last opposition to be overpowered (v. 26)
     B. The establishing of God's kingdom
        1. All that glorifies God
        2. Individually
        3. Collectively
        4. Universally
     C. The uplifting of God's son–he *must* reign
     D. The presenting to God the Father
        Note: ultimately, universally, God will be "all in all"

53

Communications and Behavior

1 Corinthians 15:29-34

Those who disbelieved in the resurrection were greatly in-fluencing the Corinthian Christians. Paul expressed his deep concern by quoting an ancient proverb: "Evil com-munications (or bad company) corrupt good manners." In our communications-conscious era, we need to remember this truth.

I. The evolution of communications
Note: "communication"–Greek *homiliai,* literally "interaction," "fellowship," or "speech"
   A. The loneliness of the individual
   B. The establishment of community
   C. The development of language
   D. The advent of media
   E. The age of electronics
   F. The fact of a "global village"

II. The effect of communications
- A. Communications and confused behavior (v. 29)
  1. Conflicting information
     a. The dead don't rise
     b. Be baptized for the dead
  2. Confused response
     a. Superficial thinking
     b. Superstitious acting
- B. Communications and courageous behavior (vv. 30–32)
  1. Undeniable communications
     a. The dead rise again
     b. Some to glory, others to condemnation
     c. Paul will arise to give account of his stewardship
  2. Unreserved application
     a. He believes what he believes
     b. He takes it to its conclusion
  3. Unrelenting determination–nothing can deter him
- C. Communications and corrupt behavior (vv. 33–34)
  1. Communication of error leading to deception
  2. Communication of evil leading to destruction
  3. Communication of emptiness leading to despair

III. The employment of communications
- A. Means of acquainting people with the truth
- B. Means of arguing against error
- C. Means of alerting people to sin
- D. Means of awaking people to righteousness

54

Life after Death

1 Corinthians 15:35-49

Paul's teaching on the resurrection of the body provoked considerable reaction. He used this reaction to develop even further his explanation of life after death.

I. Some skeptical attitudes
  A. The Pauline revelation
    1. Christ rose again (v. 20)
    2. Those "in Christ" will be raised (v. 23)
  B. The pagan reaction
    1. How can the dead rise? (v. 35)
    2. What kind of bodies will they have? (v. 35)

II. Some scriptural answers (vv. 36–49)
  A. By way of example (vv. 36–41)
    1. God's dynamic shown in the vegetable realm (vv. 36–38)
      a. The miracle of resurrection (v. 36)
      b. The miracle of transformation (v. 37)
      c. The miracle of multiplication (v. 38)

      2. God's diversity shown in the animal realm (v. 39)

      3. God's differentiation shown in the celestial realm (vv. 40–41)

        a. Celestial beings (v. 40)

        b. Terrestrial beings

        c. Celestial bodies (v. 41)

  B. By way of explanation (vv. 42–49)

      1. God's dynamic shown in changing:

        a. Corruption into incorruption (v. 42)

        b. Dishonor into glory (v. 43a)

        c. Weakness into power (v. 43b)

      2. God's diversity shown in creating:

        a. Natural body–Greek *psuchikos* (v. 44)

        b. Dishonor into glory (v. 43a)

        c. Weakness into power (v. 43b)

      3. God's differentiation shown in contrast

        a. Earthly body like Adam's (v. 47a)

        b. Heavenly body like Christ's (v. 47b)

III. Some spiritual applications (see Phil. 3:21; 1 John 3:2)

  A. Life after death is to be anticipated because it will be–

      1. Incorruptible

      2. Beautiful

      3. Powerful

      4. Spiritual

      5. Celestial

  B. Life before death is to be appreciated because it is similar, though limited

55

A Christian's Look at Death

1 Corinthians 15:50-58

Death has been shown to be 100 percent fatal. It is no respecter of persons and has little concern for its cruel consequences. It is not surprising, therefore, that "death," whilst being a stark reality, is treated by humans with a great deal of fantasy—unless the humans are Christian.

I. Christians look at death responsibly
   A. They live life in the light of death
   B. They approach death in the light of life
   C. Thus they avoid the extremes of denial or obsession

II. Christians look at death theologically
   A. The sting of death (v. 56)
     1. The sting of death is sin (see Rom. 6:23)
      a. Because sin initially caused death
      b. Because sin is judged after death
     2. The strength of sin is law (see 7:7ff.)

      3. The sting has been drawn by Christ
        a. In him the law is satisfied (see 10:4)
        b. In him sin is judged (see 8:1ff.)
   B. The "swallowing" of death (1 Cor. 15:54)
      1. The initial swallowing–Christ's resurrection
      2. The continued swallowing–those present with the Lord
      3. The final swallowing–the return of Christ
        a. The changing of the living (v. 52)–fit for the kingdom (vv. 50–52)
        b. The raising of the dead (v. 52)–equipped for eternal environment
        c. Death will then be swallowed up in victory (v. 54)

III. Christians look at death practically
   A. They face death fearlessly (v. 55)
   B. They praise God continually (v. 57)
   C. They approach service consistently (v. 58)

56

Concerning the Collection

1 Corinthians 16:1-4

The church in Jerusalem was extremely poor. Paul thought that the churches overseas should be concerned, so he organized a "collection." His teaching on the subject is invaluable to the church today.

I. The spiritual aspects of the collection
   Note: the words Paul uses to describe it
   A. Collection–Greek *logia* (v. 1)
      1. Related to *logos*–communicate, contribute
      2. Jewish background (Exod. 30:12; Neh. 10:32; Matt. 17:24)
   B. Liberality–Greek *charis* (v. 3)
      1. The attitude of God to man is *charis*
      2. The attitude of believers to God's work is *charis*
   C. Contribution–Greek *koinonia* (Rom. 15:26)
      1. Sharing with someone in something
      2. Sharing something with someone (e.g., Luke 5:7–10)

D. Relief, service—Greek *diakonia* (Acts 11:29; Rom. 15:31)
  1. Related to the idea of waiting on table (Luke 10:40; Acts 6:1)
  2. Attitude of Christ and his disciples (Luke 22:24–27)
E. Bounty—Greek *eulogia* (2 Cor. 9:5)
  1. Originally "to speak well of"; e.g., eulogize
  2. Hence "to bless" or attribute worth to
F. Alms—Greek *eleemosune* (Acts 24:17)
  1. Related to *eleos*—mercy, pity
  2. Expected by Christ (see Matt. 6:1–4)
G. Offerings—Greek *prosphora* (Acts 24:17)
  Bringing to God evidences of appreciation (see Mal. 1)

II. The practical aspects of the collection
  A. Practical attitudes
    1. Understanding the principles of the collection
    2. Undertaking the responsibility of obedience (1 Cor. 16:1)
  B. Practical actions
    1. Everybody should participate (v. 2)
    2. Participation involves preparation (v. 2)
    3. Preparation based on proportion (v. 2)
  C. Practical administration (vv. 3–4)
  D. Practical advantages
    1. God is honored
    2. Needs are met
    3. Givers are enriched

57

Local Churches and World Missions

1 Corinthians 16:5-12

Paul's ministry was so international in scope that he gave a sense of world missions to all the local churches he established. Local churches need to remember that Christ died for all and that all need to know. Therefore, our subject today is of primary importance.

  I. Local churches should understand world missions
     A. The spiritual aspects of world missions
        1. The will of the Lord (v. 7)
        2. The ways of the Lord (v. 9; see Acts 14:27; Col. 4:3)
        3. The work of the Lord (1 Cor. 16:10)
     B. The practical aspects of world missions (v. 9)
        1. The opportunities
           a. The vastness of the opportunity—"great doors"
           b. The viability of the opportunity—"effectual"
           c. The variety of the opportunity (e.g., see Acts 19:1, 8–9, 21, 30)

2. The opponents
   a. Cultural opponents (v. 9)
   b. Spiritual opponents (v. 13)
   c. Political opponents (v. 23)

II. Local churches should undergird world missionaries
   A. By meeting with them on a personal level to understand:
      1. Their personalities
         a. Paul the pioneer (1 Cor. 16:5–8)
         b. Timothy the team player (v. 11; see Acts 19:22)
         c. Apollos the articulate (1 Cor. 16:12)
      2. Their peculiarities
         a. Paul tended to be unpredictable
         b. Timothy tended to be uncomfortable
         c. Apollos tended to be unmanageable
      3. Their potentialities
         a. Paul in an explosive role
         b. Timothy in a supportive role
         c. Apollos in a creative role
   B. By ministering to them on a practical level
      1. By giving them equipment (vv. 6, 11)
      2. By giving them encouragement (vv. 10–11)
      3. By giving them refreshment (v. 18)

58

Things to Do

1 Corinthians 16:13-20

In the midst of his concluding personal remarks, Paul suddenly released a veritable barrage of instructions to the Corinthians. These imperatives are all in the present tense, which indicates that they should be regarded as ongoing instructions that should be a regular part of their lifestyle.

I. Be alert—"watch ye . . ." (v. 13)
   A. Be alert to the return of Christ (Matt. 24:42)
   B. Be alert to the resourcefulness of Satan (1 Peter 5:8)
   C. Be alert to the reasons for decay (Rev. 3:2)

II. Be stable—"stand fast . . ." (v. 13)
   A. Be stable enough to make a stand
   B. Be stable enough to maintain your stand
      1. In the faith (v. 13)
      2. In the Lord (Phil. 4:1)
      3. In the Spirit (1:2)

III. Be adult—"quit you like men . . ." (1 Cor. 16:13)
  A. Be adult in appetite (3:2)
  B. Be adult in attitude (13:11)
  C. Be adult in activity (9:25)

IV. Be strong (16:13)
  Note: may be "be strengthened"
  A. Be strong by being firmly gripped (e.g., Mark 14:51)
  B. Be strong by firmly gripping (e.g., 2 Thess. 2:15)

V. Be affectionate—"Let everything be done in love" (1 Cor. 16:14)
  A. Be loving in the handling of controversy (1 Cor. 14)
  B. Be loving in matters of conscience (1 Cor. 10)
  C. Be loving in matters of conflict (1 Cor. 5)

VI. Be submissive—"submit yourselves . . ." (16:16)
  A. By appreciating the servant attitude (v. 15)
  B. By accepting a supportive role (v. 16)
  C. By acting in a submissive manner (v. 16)

VII. Be appreciative—"acknowledge them . . ." (v. 18)
  A. Recognize the refreshers (note Matt. 11:29)
  B. Relay your appreciation

59

Maranatha

1 Corinthians 16:21-24

In the final passage of 1 Corinthians it is interesting to note that three non-English words have survived the translation. Each is important. "Maranatha" is Aramaic, "Anathema" is Greek, and "Amen" is Hebrew.

I. *Maranatha*–a word of confession
    Note: *mar* = Lord, *an* = our, *atha* = come, has come, will come
    A. A confession of incarnation–"our Lord has come"
        1. Jesus came as Lord (*mar* shows primitive teaching)
        2. Jesus came as Christ (see 1 John 4:2)
        3. Jesus should be loved for coming (1 Cor. 16:22)
    B. A confession of identification–"our Lord is present"
        1. Present as president of the church
        2. Present as dispenser of grace (v. 23)
    C. A confession of anticipation–"our Lord will come"
        1. Anticipation of termination of this era

      2. Anticipation of consummation of God's plan
      3. Anticipation of foundation of new age
    D. A confession of aspiration—"our Lord come!"
      1. Aspiration to the world to come (see Rev. 22:20)

II. *Anathema*—a word of condemnation
   Note: "devoted to deity," "for destruction" (see Josh. 6:21)
    A. The reality of divine condemnation
      1. God is the God of truth and righteousness
      2. He condemns that which is opposite
      3. Ultimately what he condemns will be destroyed (Rev. 2:27)
    B. The remedy of divine condemnation
      1. The anathema of Christ (2 Cor. 5:21)
      2. The curse of Christ (Gal. 3:13)
    C. The release from divine condemnation (Rom. 8:1)
      1. Repentance of sin
      2. Response to Christ
    D. The reminder of divine condemnation
      1. Those who love not Christ are anathema (v. 22)
      2. Those who love not Christ don't say maranatha

III. *Amen*—a word of confirmation
   Note: the acknowledgment of a word that is valid (e.g., Deut. 27:15; 1 Kings 1:36)
    A. An intelligent acknowledgment (see 1 Cor. 14:16)
    B. An involved acknowledgment
      1. Involvement in "maranatha"
      2. Involvement in "anathema"

Cassette tapes of the sermons preached from the outlines in this book are available from

TELLING THE TRUTH
P.O. Box 11
Brookfield, WI 53005